LIKE STARS IN THE HEAVENS

LIKE STARS IN THE HEAVENS

KNOWING, LIVING AND SHARING THE GOSPEL IN TODAY'S WORLD

Dean Storelli

SAMPLE

This booklet was printed in limited numbers. It is a brief selection of a larger work.

Please contact Dean Storelli (storelli@duke.edu) for ordering information.

Unless otherwise noted, all scripture quotations are taken from the New American Standard, copyright © 1960, 1962, 1963, 1968, 1971, 1972, 1973, 1975, 1977, 1995 by The Lockman Foundation.

Copyright © 2013 Dean Storelli

All rights reserved.

*Do all things without grumbling or disputing;
so that you will prove yourselves to be blameless and innocent,
children of God above reproach in the midst of a crooked and perverse
generation, among whom you appear as lights in the world....*

Philippians 2:14-15

*Those who have insight will shine brightly like the brightness of the expanse of
heaven, and those who lead the many to righteousness,
like the stars forever and ever.*

Daniel 12:3

CONTENTS

	Introduction	p. 1
1.	Laughing with Friends	p. 5
2.	Looking to Affirm	p. 16

NOTE TO READER

Some books you can just pick up and start reading anywhere. This is one of them. There is a thread you can follow as you read the chapters in order, but each chapter also stands independently.

Introduction

And a servant of the Lord must not quarrel but be gentle to all, able to teach, patient....
                                             - 2 Timothy 2:24 (NKJV)

For 2,000 years, news and stories about Jesus have been shared person-to-person and relationship-to-relationship, not by religious professionals but by "everyday people" like you and me. As Rodney Starke explains, even the great apostle Paul, who travelled broadly, did less to reach people himself then he did "as a trainer, organizer, and motivator of missionaries" (*Cities of God*, 2006, p. 134).

And what was the nature of this training? Looking at his letters, it is clear that the focus was not on making apologetic arguments but on doing good deeds, living humble lives and working at relationships. In other words, character and kindness are just as important as the words people share.

Even more clear is the idea that the advance of the gospel is not solely the responsibility of people who travel or cross cultures or boldly speak to strangers but is something everyone can be a part of in their everyday lives among co-workers, neighbors, friends and family. As Mike Shamy and Jim Peterson have described in their book, *The Insider*, Paul (and others) were counting on the people they reached to continue to spread the good news not by joining them on their travels but by living attractive lives and opening conversations with people within their own nature circles of relationships. In other words, while traveling missionaries may have brought the Gospel **to** a city, it was the task of the people to spread the Gospel **through** the city.

And until now, it has worked. Living and sharing the good news this way, the number of followers of Christ has slowly but steadily grown from a few hundred to a few thousand to billions of followers today. In Africa, South America and Asia, this pattern of growth is continuing, with the world's greatest increase in the numbers of people who claim Jesus as their Lord coming from these areas.

Tragically, in the US, Europe and Australia, this growth has come to a stop. A recent PEW Foundation survey reports that the United States is "on the verge of becoming a minority Protestant country; the number of Americans who report that they are members of Protestant denominations now stands at barely 51%" and that the fastest growing group in the US are those who are unaffiliated with any particular religion. (Available at religions.pewforum.org/report.) While single churches may be growing and some individuals may be coming to Christ, these increases can not keep up with the number of churches that are closing and the number of people who are turning away from faith. As Tim Keller puts it, here in the US most church growth is really just "Christian reconfiguration" and that the days when most people went to church and were generally prepared to hear the gospel are now "gone." (Available at movementday.com.)

There are many factors that can be taken into account to explain this stagnation: secularization, post-modernism, consumerism, moral decay and others, but the argument of this book is a simpler one: we, the followers of Christ, have largely forgotten our role - and the simple skills - that the person-to-person advance of the gospel has always depended on.

People are the Answer

As a part of an evangelical Christian organization, The Navigators, I have been trained in many outreach skills: how to draw out and explain why we need Christ using the *Bridge Illustration*, how to concisely share the story of my own coming to Christ in a 3-minute testimony, how to help a young Christian get started on their own spiritual journey by memorizing key Biblical principles (using the *Topical Memory System*) and other tools.

But the most important thing I have learned is that it is normal, everyday people that are God's "technique" for reaching the world. The thing that really counts is people **and how they carry themselves in the world**.

Paul's letters to Timothy capture this principle well. In an age of competing world views, multiple religious options, widespread promiscuity and brutal governments, Paul teaches Timothy that the key to seeing God's good news protected and shared is not a better book or a better model of presentation but the people who are carrying this message. People are the storehouses for the stories and the truths that give life and light to the world. Jesus communicated this same principle when he told his disciples that they were the salt, they were the light.

Many years ago, my friend and mentor, Gary Bradley, taught me a short list of principles that help capture the simple kind of living and communicating that people who are salt and light need. It is this list, tried and refined over the past 20 years, that this book is built around. They each captured some aspect of what it means for us to carry the Gospel in a way that is in step with Jesus and with the teachings of Paul and the other apostles. They are the "micro skills" that every follower of Christ needs to be effective as an "insider." They are principles that naturally open doors, gently deepen conversations, give joy to ourselves and others, and clearly, over time, point people to Christ.

Jesus' interaction with the woman at the well is a great example. Despite being tired and thirsty, Jesus very quickly ends up talking about the deepest things in this woman's life. After Jesus' initial request, the woman slowly opens up, begins asking her own questions and makes some startling discoveries.

How was Jesus able to transform what started as a simple request for water into something so meaningful? While many people have trouble getting into "spiritual" conversations, for Jesus, it seems so effortless.

The Way is Not Complicated

The main idea of this book is that Jesus was able to have such conversations by interacting with people in a way that is very attainable. His success was not based on special techniques or special knowledge but on an approach to life that is simple and gracious.

This book is an attempt to capture the way of life that Jesus modeled and that the apostles taught. While each idea captured in each chapter is simple to understand, most people have found that building practices such as laughing, listening and loving into our lives is not so easy. So, in each chapter you will find both a little bit of "construction" – some encouragement and ideas for living this way – and a bit of "deconstruction" (or diagnosis) of the things that keep us from living these values.

Unfortunately, some of what we need to unlearn and some of what we have forgotten comes from the misapplication of our faith. While becoming a Christian is a life-giving, growing experience, unfortunately, because we are imperfect, there are times when the *culture of Christianity* gets tainted with this imperfection. An earlier, working title of this book – "How to be human even after becoming Christian" – captures well this unfortunate reality (even if it is a bit much for a title.)

The stories here come from real life. The only changes have been in names, to protect people's privacy.

NOTES

Rodney Starke. 2006. *Cities of God: The Real Story of How Christianity Became an Urban Movement and Conquered Rome.* New York: HarperCollins.

The Pew Forum on Religion and Public Life. 2012. *Summary of Key Findings, US Religious Landscape Survey.* Available at http://religions.pewforum.org/reports.

Tim Keller. 2012. Plenary Speaker. Available at http://movementday.com/698229.ihtml.

1

Laughing with Friends

What does it mean to "participate in the Gospel"? For many people, a phrase like this one (from Philippians 1:5) brings up images of the Apostle Paul, travelling around the world, influencing every stranger he ever met.

But Paul's focus was not on recruiting people to join him in his travels or even, primarily, on asking people to copy his own pattern of movement. Instead, he was constantly teaching and reminding people about the importance of character, love and doing good in middle of the relationship people already have and in the places they already live.

In the book of Philippians, for example, Paul begins with a prayer that the lives of God's people would be full of love, wisdom, sincerity and right relationships (1:9-11). It is important, he explains, for people to conduct themselves "in a manner worthy of the gospel of Christ" and in this way to "strive" for the faith of others (1:27). After outlining how Christ's way of life should be affecting our own (Philippians 2:1-11), Paul begins to give some details:

> Do all things without grumbling or disputing; so that you will prove yourselves to be blameless and innocent, children of God above reproach in the midst of a crooked and perverse generation, among whom you appear as lights in the world. (Philippians 2:14-15)

The first thing to notice is that this call is not to certain activities (the passage begins with pulling our attention to "all things") but to doing everything we do with a certain attitude and for specific reasons. The mark of a Christian is not the types of activities that we do or don't do but the way we carry ourselves and why we carry ourselves this way. To walk through life without grumbling or complaining may sound like a fairly low standard – until you've tried it.

The second thing to notice is where this living is supposed to happen. Three times in verse 15, our place in the middle of this world is emphasized: "in the midst," "among whom" and "in the world," all demonstrating that being a Christian is something that is done out among people, out there "in" the world. Being "blameless and innocent" is something we can do every place we find ourselves (though some places are clearly easier than others.)

These two ideas together paint the picture of how God's people are to live. Like lights in the sky (the Philippians passage reminds me of Daniel 12:3), we are called in the midst of our everyday activities to follow Christ by living with a kind of grace, hope and love that is both as subtle and as attractive as stars in a dark sky.

Laughter (and Other Ways of Living in this World)

This book is built around the idea that how we live is the key to sharing Christ with others. In workshops, I talk about the principles of this kind of living using a series of Ls: live, love, laugh and others. (Such a device is good for presentations but not so good for chapter titles, I've been told.)

Laughter, our first "L," is a good topic to begin our exploration. Besides being a good sign of how we are doing with our "grumbling and complaining," laughter is also a good measure of our ability to connect to the people God has asked us to live among. Like being able to tell jokes in another language, the ability to laugh demonstrates how close we are to the people around us.

A few years ago, the link between laughter and connecting to others was driven home for me through some comments at a retreat I was leading. I was talking with a small group of people in their 20s who were starting their first real jobs, and one woman commented that "sometimes I have to bite my own tongue to keep from laughing at their jokes." The problem, once we dug into it, was not that the jokes were crude. For this young woman trying to sort out what it means to be a Christian in the workplace, the problem was that by laughing, she was afraid she might be identifying with the people around her. She was afraid her co-workers might think she was "one of them." For her, being close to people and being the same as other people was a confusing problem.

Although I think this person's response is a little extreme, I think many people have questions about just how close we are supposed to be to the people around us. In the back of our minds, we know we are suppose to be connected to the world to some extent, but how much? We may want to connect, but we may also have the feeling that it would be wrong to be "part of the group" too much or to rub shoulders too closely with people who don't know Christ. To join in the laughter, we recognize, would mean being part of the crowd. So, there is a tendency to pull back, to bite our tongues, not to laugh.

And it is this kind of hesitancy and doubt that, unfortunately, makes it hard for people to be comfortable around us. We may indeed be God's people, but being unsure or distant from others makes us a little less "human," a little less able to live the kind of lives with others that God has designed us for and called us to.

Jesus describes this kind of living as being "salt and light" (Matthew 5:13-16). It is a lifestyle that is distinct but also connected, a way of life that is different but different in a way that makes us more useful, not less. In Matthew 5, the point that Jesus makes about salt is specifically about salt's useful role in making things taste better. (Most Bibles translate the word here as "taste" or "flavor.") This is a distinction that is attractive.

In the same passage, when he is talking about light, Jesus focuses on the need to be out in the open. Like salt, light is also meant for the good of others, but it can only fulfill this role when it is visible to others. Eugene Peterson's *The Message* translation of the Bible captures these idea beautifully:

> "Let me tell you why you are here. You're here to be salt-seasoning that brings out the God-flavors of this earth…. You're here to be light, bringing out the God-colors in the world. God is not a secret to be kept. We're going public with this, as public as a city on a hill. If I make you light-bearers, you don't think I'm going to hide you under a bucket, do you? I'm putting you on a light stand. Now that I've put you there on a hilltop, on a light stand—shine! Keep open house; be generous with your lives. By opening up to others, you'll prompt people to open up with God, this generous Father in heaven." (Matthew 5:13-16, MSG)

Just as "saltiness" is meant to enhance flavor and brightness is meant to aid travel, so our purpose on this earth is not to live in isolation from others but to take full part in God's love and care for all people:

> "But I say to you, love your enemies and pray for those who persecute you, so that you may be sons of your Father who is in heaven; for He causes His sun to rise on the evil and the good, and sends rain on the righteous and the unrighteous. For if you love those who love you, what reward do you have? Do not even the tax collectors do the same? If you greet only your brothers, what more are you doing than others? Do not even the Gentiles do the same? Therefore you are to be perfect, as your heavenly Father is perfect." (Matthew 5:44-48)

What is Laughter All About?

What, then, is the role of laughter in all this? A quick search of the Old and New Testaments generates a good sized list of examples of laughing and rejoicing. These passages demonstrate that laughter can have a variety of meanings. Here, I'd like to explore two ways that laughter is a part of how we are suppose to be living in and impacting the world around us.

Laughter: A Bond in Relationships

First, laughter is about relationships. Like the young woman in the workshop who was afraid to laugh with her colleagues, we know that laughter has a way of tying people together. And this kind of close association, especially through laughter, is explicitly commanded in the Bible.

Throughout the New Testament, Christians are called to join in the pain and the joy of others. Romans 12:15, 1 Corinthians 12:26 and Philippians 2:18 are just three examples. Among them, the passage in Romans implies the widest application. Romans 12:15 tell us to "rejoice with those who rejoice and weep with those who weep." The context of the passage (vv. 14-21) makes it clear that this passage is not about how believers are supposed to treat other believers but about how Christ's followers are suppose to live within the community of all people. The passage is about how we are to treat "anyone" and calls us to do "what is right" in everyone's eyes (v. 17).

To understand the role that this kind of connecting can have, I'd like to look at the Bible's first, and perhaps most revealing, story about laughter: the story of Abraham and Sarah and how they laughed at God.

For most of his life, Abraham lived with some extravagant promises made by God: "I will make you a great nation. I will bless you and make your name great.... In you all of the families of the earth will be blessed" (Genesis 12:1-3). But for years, there was nothing. Yes, there were some military victories and the rescue of his nephew Lot, but there was no heir, no child through whom the promises could be fulfilled. And even though God kept reminding Abraham, Abraham had trouble believing, at one point taking matters into his own hands by having a child with another woman.

It is in the middle of one of these conversations with God about his future (Genesis 17:1-20) that Abraham laughs. He has just been given a new name by God, instructed regarding circumcision and promised children and great blessing, and he laughs at the very idea of his wife bearing a child (17:17). He was an old man, his wife was old and she had never been able to conceive. His laughter does not seem to have been in defiance of God – he had fallen on his face before God, not daring to even mention his doubts out loud. But his shocked, overwhelmed, incredulous heart could not hold back an unbelieving laugh, followed by the suggestion that God let the blessing flow through Ishmael, the child he had fathered with another woman.

God's response is a simple "no" and repetition of the promise to give a child through Sarah.

Soon after, Sarah had a chance to hear this same message (chapter 18), and her response was also to laugh. This time, God had something to say about it, and Sarah was frightened. She tried to deny laughing, but she had been heard, the message of her laughter clearly communicated. Even so, God again confirms his promise to give them a child.

And how does this story end? With more laughter, but this time, for a very different reason. Having finally given birth to the promised child, Sarah's response is a humble, overjoyed acceptance of God's blessing:

> God has made laughter for me; everyone who hears will laugh with me. (Genesis 21:6)

We must be careful not to make one story say too much, but I think it is safe to say that even this one story demonstrates that laughter can be the heart's deepest cry, that it can represent years of doubt and failure, that it can be the expression of a heart that is too full or too hurt to believe any more, and yet, still struggles to believe. And isn't this place of honest longing exactly where we want to be with our friends, especially those who know little about God or are struggling to believe?

A quick survey of the Bible teaches that laughter is tied closely to faith, and therefore closely tied to how we want to connect to others. Laughter can communicate the confidence that comes from trusting God (Job 5:22, Proverbs 31:25) and the joy that comes even in the midst of sorrow (Proverbs 14:13). Expanding our survey to include the idea of rejoicing demonstrates this same pattern: laughter and rejoicing communicate deep human emotions, and God's people are expected to rejoice both as a form of worship[1] and as a way to connect to others. In other words, laughter is a part of life, especially a life of faith, and unless we are

---

[1] For a few examples of the role of rejoicing in worship, see Leviticus 23:40 and Deuteronomy 12:7, 12:12, 14:26, 26:11.

willing to walk with people through both their tears and joys, it is unlikely we will ever be invited to share in their joy at the discovery of the God who is renown for turning tears into laughter. Laughter is a gift that crosses the gulf that keeps people feeling isolated and alone. It offers a glimpse of hope. It is a welcomed new flavor, a cup of cold water in an otherwise dry land. Our laughter reminds us that love is possible and connection available. It is not something we reserve for people who "deserve" it, but a gift we give out broadly.

The Joy of Living
The second way that laughter is a part of how we are called to live in this world is the simple joy of living. To a watching world, our laughter and joy point to the goodness and strength of God (Psalm 126).

The Bible does not teach that there are no good things in life. It teaches that all good things come from God and that no good thing comes to us apart from God (James 1:17). Perhaps the problem is that we, at times, forget to see God's hand in the good that is around us. We sense only "guilty pleasure" in that great cup of coffee, a rich slice of cheesecake or the good tired of a good workout or a job well done not because there is guilt in the gift but because we have forgotten the source of the gift. In the absence of a good explanation – "praise God for this good gift!" – we assume there is only a bad explanation. Somehow, we get everything backwards and instead of recognizing that the reason we are enjoying something is because God has provided, we jump to the conclusion that if we are enjoying something, it must be wrong. Of course, there are empty pleasures that we should reject, but it seems that many within the body of Christ have let this proper attitude towards bad things lead us to feeling guilty or suspicious even of good things. This is not holiness.

The book of Ecclesiastes is in some ways a master thesis on pleasure. After exploring the limits of wisdom, chapter 2 shifts to a look at pleasure. And although the writer states that there are limits to how long pleasure can last, he still concludes that "there is nothing better for a man than to eat and drink and tell himself that his labor is good" (Ecclesiastes 2:24, and repeated in 3:12-13 and 5:18-19). The problem with pleasure is not that we enjoy it but that we can forget where it is coming from. The problem is not that we laugh but that at times we forget why we are laughing, and in forgetting, we feel guilty. The solution, therefore, is not to stop laughing but to start remembering.

If we truly believe that there is one God of all creation – and this creation includes human beings and the many talents and drives he has filled us with – then pursuing God should not be seen as automatically opposed to pursuing our passions (Psalm 37:4). God's desire is to fulfill our desires: he planted them there. Like the great runner, Eric Liddell, when we run (or fish, or bake, or paint, or rest, or teach, or design, or build, or shop, or listen, or speak, or craft a budget, or operate out of any of the good abilities God has given us) we, too, should "feel his pleasure."

Too often, Christians have become convinced that if they enjoy something, it must be sin. If that is the case, what does it mean that history is headed toward a wedding party (Revelation 19:7-8), that we are commanded or given examples of rejoicing over 50 times in the New Testament, that someday God will "wipe away every tear from their eyes; and there will no longer be *any* death; there will no longer be *any* mourning, or crying, or pain" (Revelation 21:4)? If the full enjoyment of life is something we are all heading towards, and if "eternal life" is a path we have already taken our first step on, shouldn't laughter and joy be a part of our lives now? The joyful pursuit of our passions should be a part of our lives. Enjoying what we do should not be a cause for guilt, not by itself.

Reasons Not to Laugh

There are, of course, times when we shouldn't laugh. The apostle James, who said that "every good thing given and every perfect gift is from above" (James 1:17) also warned us not to be "carried away" by our desires (v. 14). Enjoyment and the pursuit of our passions, like everything else, is something we are supposed to manage. A good example of this would be choosing not to laugh when laughter is only meant to hurt someone or as a way to hide.

And, here, in my opinion, is where true holiness comes into play. Our calling requires us to live in a delicate balance. We are to be distinct but not so different that we can no longer be understood. This tension means that we will rarely have the option of making moral decisions with a "meat cleaver." Outside of commands that truly are universal (things like no stealing, no lying and others), most of the decisions we have to make are not primarily matters of "always yes" or "always no." To find God's way will require both some experience (that is why Hebrews 5:14 talks about having our "senses trained to discern good and evil") and some thoughtful reflection.

The "simple" approach is to outline a personal set of "scruples" (behavioral rules) and then stick by them without question no matter what happens. But when this happens in areas of our lives that are inappropriate for such simplicity, we are actually shutting the door on God's interaction and saying "no" to God's wisdom in the present moment. The decision we made at some prior point in our life may have been exactly right for that situation, but this history does not mean it will be right in every situation.

Knowing when to laugh, like all areas of life, is something that may at times need a little "homework" and introspection, but as we grow into maturity, we can expect that more and more, God will guide us into all truth and appropriate freedom. Though earlier in my walk with God, for example, I may have hesitated to tease someone, I'm pretty convinced that my brother-in-law's "love language" is teasing. Needling him back is one of the best ways I can tell him he's okay.

The Joy of Christmas

Jesus is God's ultimate answer to the question of where and how his people are supposed to be living. He is both the solution for our failures and our model for what being human is all about.

Our introduction to Christ on earth – and the inauguration of this new way of "being human" – is Christmas. The whole story is wrapped in words of the deepest joy and intimate connections. It was announced, as Linus so famously reminds us in *It's Christmas Charlie Brown*, with this message: "Glory to God in the highest, and on earth peace, good will toward men" (Luke 2:14, KJV).

The birth of God's only son **as one of us means** that being human is, and has always been meant to be, a good and joyful thing. It means that God, despite all of our sins and shortcomings, wants to live in our midst. People love Christmas, I think, because of the joy and hope that God's desire to be with us communicates. Christmas gives us a good taste of what it means to walk hand-in-hand with God, and the book of Revelation promises even more. From the throne, we hear:

> "Look! Look! God has moved into the neighborhood, making his home with men and women! They're his people, he's their God. He'll wipe every tear from their eyes. Death is gone for good—tears gone, crying gone, pain gone—all the first order of things gone." (Revelation 21:3-4, MSG)

This is the fulfillment of a long promise. It is the completion of a task assigned a long, long time ago. After the fall and our separation from God, the nation of Israel was called to bless the nations and show humanity the way back, a duty they failed to achieve until their "greatest son," Jesus came to us. Through his life, death and resurrection, through what he taught and what he did for others, through all of these, he blessed us and restored us to God. Jesus was born for more than dying. He was born to model a way of life, to die for our failures and to write into history a new path to God.

What a privilege it is to be allowed to enter into the joy of God and into the laughter of others!

QUESTIONS

1. Think about the people around you everyday. Who among them laughs well and for good reasons? Is there any reason why you couldn't or shouldn't laugh with them?

2. Think about the times you laugh. Why are you laughing and what do you think your laughter might be communicating? Is that ok?

3. In general, do you think you laugh enough? Do any of the reasons for not laughing talked about in this chapter apply to you? I.e., are you reluctant to be "part of the gang" or do you feel nervous about enjoying life "too much"?

EXERCISE

Make a list with room to add some comments. Divide the list into three sections: people, problems, passions.

People

Problems

Passions

In the "People" section, list people you would like to be closer to. Under "Problems," list things you are currently worried about. Under "Passions," list aspects of your job, hobbies, things that you own, etc., that you almost feel (or actually do feel) guilty for liking so much.

After writing down a few items for each section, make some notes.

- For the people, list some things you like about that person, things that make it easy for you to enjoy being around them. Take a minute to thank God for this person and these traits he has given them.

- For the problems, are there any promises you feel God has made that might help you worry less?

- For the passions, evaluate: are these things God has given you? Is there a specific reason why you shouldn't enjoy them? Are there specific reasons why you should be thankful for them? Spend a little time praying.

RESOURCES

Two Bible studies that take an in-depth look at what it means to live in the world and share the Gospel, *Separation or Among* and *Knowing, Living and Sharing the Gospel*, can be found at human365.org.

2

Looking to Affirm

Despite what the children's rhyme says, by now most of us have come to the sad realization that in addition to the damage that "sticks and stones" can do, words can also deeply hurt us. Most of us can remember times when we were called names or were yelled at, often with the worst damage wrapped up in the expression on the face of the person delivering these harsh words.

On the other hand, most of us, hopefully, can also remember kind words, things that went deep into our hearts – deeper than compliments – because they *said something positive about who we are*. For some of us, these moments are the most powerful turning points in our lives. They have made us who we are today. I know that it is true for me.

Looking to Agree

Unfortunately, there are things about "being Christian" that can lead us to being very reluctant to offer praise, give a compliment or acknowledge the good in people's lives. It seems like some of us have been trained to find what we disagree with instead how to look for common ground. "Speaking the truth in love" sometimes becomes an excuse to confront people with what we think we know, what we assume we see or what we assume is our responsibility to address.

My friend, let's call him Brandon, shares this story about learning to affirm his mom. In college, he became much more serious about his faith but also much more critical about his mom's. For years, he was afraid to compliment his mom for fear that she might think he was "condoning" what he saw as her lack of faith. So, instead of giving praise or even communicating appreciation for all that she had done for him, he held back.

But eventually, he took the risk and started to communicate the things he saw in her life that he was thankful for: her perseverance in troubled times, the lessons she taught him about hard work, her sensitivity in relationships, her efforts to trust God the best way she knew how. Suddenly, instead of being her adversary, Brandon was now his mom's friend. He became a support for her in her own journey of faith. Instead of fighting about what was wrong or absent from her life, they began to build together on all that was good.

In my own life, I have seen this same pattern: the more we can affirm, the more people are willing to let us in and let us help. My friend Mike has been all over the map spiritually. At one point when he was very confused about what he believed, mad at God and not sure what the Bible was all about. In the middle of this struggle, he decided that he shouldn't come to any of our campus meetings any more, at least not until he worked out some of his questions. I did not think this was a good idea, and it would have been easy for me to find things to disagree with: some of the struggles had to do with misunderstandings of the Bible, his decision to withdraw left him isolated from getting any kind of help, there were other people who were depending on him and his leadership within the group, etc. But instead of arguing with him (he was clearly coming to me just to inform me of his decision, not to ask advice) I decided to affirm him for what I could. Listening to his reasons for wanting to drop out of the group, I could tell that for him, being a part of the group while having all these doubts was an issue of integrity. I shared with him this conclusion and told him that I thought he was a man of honor and someone who valued honesty. Mike had been feeling pretty nervous, I think, about telling me what he wanted to do, but by agreeing with what I could, we kept our relationship on a good foundation. I asked Mike if he wanted to continue to talk about these things. He said yes, and today Mike and I are still good friends and continue having great discussions about the ups and downs of life and faith. Eventually, he worked out those initial doubts and is doing well today. Though the road was rocky, he continues to be a great leader and a support to many others on their own walk with God. Affirmation wasn't the whole answer to his troubles, but it kept the door open during a critical turning point.

The principle here is not to be "nice" for the sake of being nice or to avoid conflict at all cost but to **look harder** than we usually do. In almost every conversation, there are things that we can agree with and things that we can disagree with. By focusing on what we disagree with, we put ourselves in an adversarial position with our friends and can end up in a lot of fights. But by focusing on what we agree with, we build trust. We strengthen the relationship to the point where it can bear some disagreement. When we have spent time affirming people, they know we care and that we are not simply out to fix them.

I see the apostle Paul urging us to live this kind of lifestyle. He urged Timothy not to be "argumentative but a gentle listener and a teacher who keeps cool" (2 Timothy 2:22-25, MSG). To me, part of this gentleness is looking for what I can agree with first. In his letter to the Romans, Paul writes that we should laugh with our friends who are laughing and cry with our friends who are crying. We should try to get along with everybody. We should try to make peace (Romans 12:14-18). These are not personality traits that some people have and some people don't (though some people are clearly more easy going than others.) These are the values and priorities that Paul says we need as we go out into the world. This is how we are supposed to live. It doesn't mean never saying hard things, but it means looking, whenever we can, first for what we can agree with.

I was recently in a conversation with a young woman who was having some trouble in a relationship, and I spent a long time just listening. (The topic of listening and affirmation are very closely tied together – it is only after you've spent some time listening and learning from someone that you will know enough to affirm them.) As I listened, it was clear that she was working hard to make a good decision. The first thing I did was tell her what a good job I thought she was doing. She was not doing everything right, but it was obvious she was trying to treat her friend with real respect and trying to be wise about the whole situation. After taking the time to affirm her for everything positive, I also brought up a few things that I thought she was missing and some new ways of seeing a couple of things. This opportunity came after listening and affirming.

Joining God

In telling a story like the one above, it is important to point out that affirmation is not just a "setup" for correcting people. All by itself, affirmation has tremendous value. It may be the most powerful thing we do.

One way to define affirmation is *naming things that exists but have not yet been revealed*.[1] God, of course, can create out of nothing and can speak order into chaos. But as he has done in many areas of life, God has given us an ability similar (though more limited) to his own. The English word that describes what God does in full and what we can do in part is "affirmation," and it gets at this idea fairly well, but the New Testament word, "logomen" (related to the Greek word for speak, "logos"), hints at even more. "Logomen" is most often translated "say," but it is also the word that Paul uses when he says that God "worded" Abraham as righteous. God was not simply describing something that already existed and was not simply creating something new (though God can do so whenever he likes). Instead, he was *affirming* something (i.e., seeing something as well as nudging it along) that was just emerging in Abraham: faith! In the paradox of faith and free will, God was both seeing something in Abraham and creating something that did not yet exist.

Remarkably, people, within our own spheres, can participate in this same kind of creating. For example, when a father or mother look at a young son or daughter, they can either see a small child or they can "see" the man or woman this child will become. If they can see the man or woman the child is becoming, and then say something about it, that's affirmation. Here's a story from my own

---

[1] This definition and the activity at the end of the chapter come from Gary Bradley.

family. A few years ago, we loaded up the car and drove down to Florida. When we got there, it took many trips up and down the stairs to get everything out of the car and up to our 3rd floor hotel room. The last item was a large cooler, maybe 3 ft. wide, and heavy. But just as I was going downstairs to get it, up comes my 13-year-old son carrying it by himself. I looked at him and smiled and said, "James, that's a man's job. Good work." Now, obviously, my 13-year-old son was not a full-grown man, and he couldn't, at that time, carry things as well as I could. But do you see what happened there? By affirming the man that he was becoming, I actually helped spur on the process. I gave him a little bit of encouragement along the path God had already laid out for him.

I saw a painting once that expresses this idea well. It pictured a seed that has sprouted and is sending out its first tender shoot and one unformed leaf – but it still has not yet broken through the surface. Almost anybody walking along would just see a lump of dirt, a bump on the ground. But what we really have here is life about to break forth. A wise farmer "affirms" that seed by watering it and waiting for it to grow. He trusts in what he can not yet see and acts as if it were already there.

And this is what we can do with the people around us. When we see God beginning to move in their lives, we can affirm this movement. We can name people's positive actions or good values for what they are: gifts from God. Whether our affirmation is direct – "hey, what you just did is a God thing!" – or indirect, what we are doing is helping people know that this thing that is happening in their life is good, and ultimately, we may win the chance to tell them that it is from God. In fact, it could be argued that as followers of God, this is our most sacred duty. As God's priests (1 Peter 2:9), we are called to bring attention to the things God is doing all through the world, and by noticing and naming them for what they are, we help in our own small way these things come into being. We join God in His creative work of making people everywhere into all that we are meant to be. If we, who are growing more and more to see the world through the eyes of faith, do not do this work, who else is there?

A karate dojo attracts all kinds of people. Yes, it does attract parents and their kids looking for something new, but also draws a good number of the "rough-and-tumble" crowd: ex-military who know how to fight, people who look like they are looking for fight and people who have definitely already been in a few fights. Over the past couple of years, I've been becoming friends with one of these tough characters. He is kind of gruff. It looks like he's been in a few scrapes in his life – one day, I actually saw him pin another man to the ground with just his thumb – but I have also see him take friends out to dinner, tell someone who's had too much that they need to quit drinking and give a poor high school student with no career skills a break by offering him a job. And when I see him do these things, I tell him so. I tell him he is a good man. I tell him he has a good heart. And you know what? I think I am helping him.

People have told me that I am good at this, at finding what people are doing right and being patient with what they are doing wrong. To the extent that it is true, I have to thank God for it. But I also have to admit that it is something I have had to work at. I am not naturally an easy-going, positive person. But because I believe that this process of agreeing with all we can is part of how God wants us to live in the world, it is a pattern I have tried to build in my life – and I think it is something others can do, too.

Why Not?

If affirmation is so powerful, why don't we do it more often? Here are four ideas that can hold us back.

Q: Won't I be Condoning Somebody's Sinful Life?
A: No.

Brandon has told me that fear of condoning his mother's life was the main reason he did not want to say anything positive to his mother. He was afraid that by affirming or complimenting *anything* about her, he would be working against the "gospel" and her need to be reconciled to God.

This is a horrible misunderstanding on several levels. First, though the idea that we all "fall short of the glory of God" (Romans 3:23) is indeed a critical part of what people need to come understand about themselves and about God, it is nowhere in the Bible mandated that this one point of the broad sweep of the "good news" is the one-and-only starting point for every conversation about God and faith. There are many, many ways to talk about the one, true God, and there are many conversations in the Bible where other messages apart from sin and the need for reconciliation come first.

Titus chapters 2 and 3 is an interesting example. In chapter 2, Paul walks us through all kinds of relationships. In chapter 3:1-2, he sums up his advice about these relationships with a reminder "to be ready for every good deed, to malign no one, to be peaceable, gentle, showing every consideration for all."

Why should we live this way? Paul explains that this "kindness" approach was at the heart of Jesus' appearance (Titus 2:11). Titus 3:4-7 outlines the pattern this way:

> But when the kindness of God our Savior and His love for mankind appeared, He saved us, not on the basis of deeds which we have done in righteousness, but according to His mercy, by the washing of regeneration and renewing by the Holy Spirit, whom He poured out upon us richly through Jesus Christ our Savior, so that being justified by His grace we would be made heirs according to the hope of eternal life.

Throughout his life, Jesus performed multiple good deeds, shared multiple encouraging words and came alongside all kinds of people, and almost all of the time, this affirmation came well before there was any conversation about sin. His kindness, mercy, encouragement, teaching and gentle nudging of people towards change came not because there was nothing wrong with people. Paul states that Jesus came to us in kindness *despite* our lack of goodness (see Titus 3:3 and 3:5). And it is this pattern leading with grace that we are called to imitate: just as God worked with us and spoke "peace" to us long before any real changes came in our own lives, so God wants us to speak peace to others.

This is not to say that we never talk to people about sin. Sin is definitely something that people eventually do have to come to understand. And sometimes, confronting someone with their sin may even be the best first step. But the lesson of Christ's appearance on earth and the example that Paul and others urge us to imitate is to love and affirm first, even when we can see much that is not good.

Q: Isn't it Dangerous to Give People Too Many Compliments?
A: Yes, but...

Affirmation does not mean giving compliments. Compliments are much easier to give than affirmation. A compliment praises somebody for something they did or congratulates them for something they achieved, but affirmation goes much deeper than that. Affirmation speaks to a person's identity. More than admiration for something somebody did, affirmation tells a person who they are. For example, when my kids were little, if I saw one of my sons share a toy with my daughter, I could say, "That was really nice of you," and that would be a compliment. It is praise for a good act. But over time, as I see him do this more than once, I could say to him, "David, you have a good heart. You have a heart that wants to share. I like that." That is affirmation. I am speaking to my son's identity.

Compliments and affirmation can both be good things. But you have to be careful with compliments. If compliments only highlight somebody's performance, it can create pressure: "I just got a compliment for sharing. Now I have to keep doing that." We have to be careful with compliments and make sure we are not creating a performance environment. Affirmation helps avoid that. It does not praise somebody for what they did but smiles at who they are.

The other difference between compliments and affirmation is that compliments have to use words, but affirmation can come in many forms: time together, a reward or even an approving look. Assigning someone a task, in recognition of the kind of person someone is growing into, can be a type of affirmation.

Q: What Am I Suppose to Say?
A: It depends. Who are you talking to?

There are few words that are more empty than a "canned" compliment, one that you can tell somebody tells everybody. Getting to know a person well enough to say something that is especially true about them does not have to take very much time, but it will take some attention to an area that we are not often trained in: we must learn to pay attention not only to our message (or even to ourselves as messengers) but to our audience and to what the person in front us is ready and able to hear.

Most of the time, when we are thinking about presenting the

Gospel to someone (or for that matter, almost any kind of communication), we mostly think – and sometimes only think – about the message itself. But as Charles Kraft, in his book *Communicating Jesus' Way*, explains, in communication there are always three components: the person sending the message, the message itself and the person receiving the message. Most of us have been taught that the most important thing to concentrate on is the message: no matter what, we need to get that clear.

But another thing that Jesus' appearance teaches us (in addition to God's deep love and kindness), is that both the messenger and the audience are equally as important. Think about it: isn't the kind of life Jesus lived also important? Doesn't Christ's character make it easier to understand and believe his message?

And isn't it amazing that God, who could have picked any form for communicating with us, picked the form that was most like us, the form, to be exact, that was us? Christ's birth was not convenient for him, it was not for his benefit. It was for us.

And among all the things that God could have begun with, he began with a comforting word, "do not be afraid," and with actions and words that show us that there are things that he is pleased about (see Luke 2:8-14). God's whole approach to Jesus' appearance on earth shows tremendous sensitivity to the needs of the audience.

Kraft, who was a missionary and teacher for most of his life, calls this kind of communication "receptor-centered" communication. Receptor orientation means our goal is not simply to *deliver* the right message, but to have it *believed*. It means we work not to make ourselves look good or even, primarily, to deliver an abundance of correct information, but to deliver effective communication, or as Paul says in Ephesians 4:29, a "nutritious" word, the kind that "is good for edification according to the need of the moment, so that it will give grace to those who hear." According to Paul, this "word" is tailored to meet the needs of the exact person we are talking to.

Affirmation is an important part of this simple, personal, effective, needed-now communication. It works not only to inform but to transform. It is almost unbelievable that we can have this kind of influence, but it is this kind of influence that passages like Ephesians 4:29 say we are suppose to have. The word "edify" literally means "to build," and that is what affirmation does: it joins

God in building up another human being by saying to that person something about their true identity.

Throughout his life, Jesus consistently tailored his message to fit his audience, beginning very often with affirmation. Some of Christ's first recorded words are in John, chapter 1. At this point, Jesus has started his teaching career and is now inviting a few people to join him. How does he do it? In his invitation Peter, John 1:42 says that, first, Jesus "looked at him," and then he gave him a new name, "Rock," speaking directly to his identity and affirming Peter's strength. (Knowing the rest of the story, couldn't Jesus just as accurately have named him "Reckless" or "Failure"?) Likewise, Jesus' first words to Nathan are a strong affirmation of Nathan's honesty, and Nathan's first response is to wonder how this man could know him so well (see John 1:48).

Some of Jesus' last words are recorded in Acts and in Revelation. In Acts, though he has some difficult news for Paul, he also affirms (through Ananias) that God has some good work for him to do (Acts 8:15-19). In Revelation, Jesus speaks to 7 communities, always saying something positive, usually right at the beginning.

Passage	Community	Affirmation
2:2-3	Ephesus	"I know your deeds and your toil and your perseverance…"
2:9	Smyrna	"I know your tribulation (but you are rich)…"
2:13	Pergamum	"I know where you dwell…and you hold fast My name and did not deny My faith even in the days of Antipas, My witness, My faithful one…"
2:19	Thyatira	"I know your deeds, and your love and faith and service and that your deeds of late are greater than at first…"
3:4	Sardis	Christ does not begin with affirmation, but after some hard words adds, "But you have a few people in Sardis who have not soiled their garments; and they will walk with Me in white, for they are worthy."
3:8	Philadelphia	"Behold, I have put before you an open door which no one can shut, because you

		have a little power, and have kept My word, and have not denied My name."
3:19	Laodicea	Here, after delivering some hard words, Jesus reassures his love and explains why: "Those whom I love, I reprove and discipline; therefore be zealous and repent."

Can you imagine being a small community of believers and hearing that Christ has delivered such words? That he has spoken positively about your specific group to no less than the Apostle John, who at the time of writing Revelation was a beloved elder statesman of the church? Even though followed in most cases by some "areas for improvement," these affirmations had the power to mark someone for life, to carry them through many ups and downs. They are still powerful today.

Q: Um, Is There Really Anything Good to Say?
A: Plenty.

The final key to affirmation is believing that there is *actually something good* that can be said. Though I will go into more detail in Chapter 10, "Latent," let me just say here that none of this book will make sense (perhaps it has not been making sense so far) unless you can agree that human beings, despite their failures, carry in themselves some echo of God. In fact, if we are honest about it, aren't there very many people who seem to be quite good, even without God?

This idea is not some "new age" philosophy. It is the fact of Genesis. The story of the Bible is that all people were created in God's image and that despite the fall, all people still bear some resemblance to God. Jesus came not to deny this image but to restore it.

Aleksandr Solzhenitsyn, who spent 8 years in a Russian gulag, had this to say about what he learned there about human nature:

> Gradually it was disclosed to me that the line separating good and evil passes not through states, nor between classes, nor between political parties either – but right through every human heart – and

through all human hearts. This line shifts. Inside us, it oscillates with the years. And even within hearts overwhelmed by evil, one small bridgehead of good is retained (*The Gulag Archipelago*).

It is this "small bridgehead" that we are looking for. The fact that we see goodness in all people should not be a challenge to our faith but an confirmation of it. It supports the idea that God made everyone and that his craftsmanship is good, strong and lasting, able to overcome even our own rebellion and apathy.

Without this basic understanding that there is good in all people and that all people have the potential for growth and change, most of the advice I have given so far in the book really does not make sense. If people are only "all good" or "all evil" (or in other words, if there are only "good Christians" and bad everyone else) then there is no way we should be laughing, listening, learning and leaning on these purely bad influences.

But my experience has been that when I look, believing that it is there, I find good. There has to be. God's work is not so easily undone.

So, Just Look

All the stories in the world can never replace experience, so I am going to make a request: just try it. Just try to look, and see what you find. If you pay attention to the people around you, looking for what is good, I think you will gain all the proof you need.

Questions

- What do you think about this idea of affirmation? Does it seem dangerous? Freeing? How does it challenge the way you usually think?

- What arguments do you find yourself raising as you read this chapter? Where do these arguments come from?

- What experience do you have with trying to affirm others? What makes it easy? What makes it difficult? Is there anything you could do to move forward?

- Think of a time when you really "blew it" – for example, you tried to say the right thing and the whole conversation blew up and then you felt terrible about yourself. Afterwards, how might affirmation have helped? What could have been said?

Bible study/discussion

1. Read through John 4:7-42, looking for examples of affirmation.
2. Look at Ephesians 1:4-13 and quickly identify things that God says are true about you. Can you hear God saying these things to you? What does that feel like?
3. In *A Wind in the Door* (the sequel to Madeleine L'Engle's *A Wrinkle in Time*), one of the key lessons the hero needs to learn is how to look past what is superficial and past her own personal dislikes to "name" and thereby restore a man she doesn't respect. In the book, the most evil power in the universe seeks just the opposite: to unmake the world by "unnaming" its inhabitants. What other works of fiction (TV, movies, books, etc.) contain or are centered on this theme of knowing and affirming?

Exercise

Look again at our definitions:

A compliment is an expression of praise, admiration or congratulation. Compliments can take many forms: telling someone "good job" or "thank you," commenting on someone's appearance or writing a note to thank or congratulate someone for doing something especially well. For many of us, giving and receiving compliments is an everyday thing. For others, it is awkward to receive a compliment, so they simply nod and shuffle on their way.

Affirmation is to bring to light what God has said is true about someone – even though it may not be seen at the moment. It starts with noticing what is just below the surface in someone's life, something that is emerging in their character or identity, and then nudging the process along through the power of affirmation to transform. It is a form of creation at work.

In pairs (if possible, with people you know) try giving a compliment (i.e. "Nice shirt!") Then, try affirming ("One thing I really appreciate about you is your patience. I have seen you....") After taking turns, talk about what it was like: which was harder to do? Why? What did it feel like on the receiving end?

ABOUT THE AUTHOR

Dean Storelli has been on staff with the Navigators since 1990 and has served in Japan and the US. He also teaches writing at Duke University's Sanford School of Public Policy. He can be contacted at storelli@duke.edu.

Made in the USA
Charleston, SC
21 January 2013